Walking Down the Path of Life

My Spiritual Journey

Many Blessings!

Helen V. Dugan

Walking Down the Path of Life
My Spiritual Journey
Copyright © 2014 Helen V. Dugan

Published by LuLu Press, Inc.
Raleigh, North Carolina USA
Visit our website:
www.lulu.com

ISBN 978-304-75553-7

Printed in the United States of America

*Special thanks to the
Holy Spirit for giving me
the courage needed to
share my testimony and
the Truth of God's Word,
The Good News
which is the
Power of the Gospel,
for such a time as this.*

Contents

God gave me a wake up call that changed my life forever...

I've been given the privilege to share with you a wonderful testimony given to me back in November of 1997, by the Holy Spirit. Through this experience I have chosen to surrender my life and asked Him to use me for His glory.

Jesus wants me to share with you, and as many people who will listen, that He loves you and is coming back very soon.

God wants to set you free but that freedom can only be found in the Truth of God's Word.

May God richly bless you.

Helen

Walking down the path of life is a journey.
There is a beginning and an end.
When I chose to begin a spiritual journey I
needed to make choices.

Choices are not always easy but when I began
reading and studying scripture, I discovered a
wonderful treasure! The truth about something
determines whether you're on the right path. By
the guidance of the Holy Spirit I began to find the
purpose for my life.

To me, the most important choice or decision I
will ever make is where I am going to spend
eternity. Scripture says that God is the Creator
of His Creation!

In God's eyes everyone has worth and value.
Through God's Word I realized that God not only
knows me but loves me, unconditionally.

The title of my book is,

*Walking Down the Path of Life
My Spiritual Journey*

"For You created my inter most being; You knit me together in my mother's womb. I praise You because I am fearfully and wonderfully made; Your works are wonderful.

I know that full well. My frame was not hidden from You when I was made in the secret place, when I was woven together in the depths of the earth. Your eyes saw my unformed body; all the days ordained for me were written in your book before one of them came to be."

Psalms 139:13-16

"For I know the plans I have for you," declares the LORD, "plans to prosper you and not harm you, plans to give you hope and a future."

Jeremiah 29:11

The Parable of the Sower

A sower went out to sow.

And it happened, as he sowed, that some seed fell by the wayside; and the birds of the air came and devoured it.

Some fell on stony ground, where it did not have much earth; and immediately it sprang up because it had no depth of earth. "But when the sun was up it was scorched, and because it had no root it withered away. And some seed fell among thorns; and the thorns grew up and choked it, and it yielded no crop.

But other seed fell on good ground and yielded a crop that sprang up, increased and produced:
some thirty-fold, some sixty, and some a hundred."
And He said to them, "He who has ears to hear, let him hear!"

The Purpose of the Parables

But when He was alone, those around Him with the twelve asked Him about the parable, And He said to them, "To you it has been given to know the mystery of the kingdom of God; but to those who are outside, all things come in parables,

"So that seeing they may see and not perceive, and hearing they may hear and not understand; Lest they should turn, And their sins be forgiven them."

The Parable of the Sower Explained

And He said to them, "Do you not understand this parable? How then will you understand all the parables?"

The sower sows the word.

"And these are the ones by the wayside where the word is sown. When they hear, Satan comes immediately and takes away the word that was sown I their hearts."

"These likewise are the ones sown on stony ground who, when they hear the word, immediately receive it with gladness; and they have no root in themselves, so endure only for a time. Afterward, when tribulation or persecution arises for the word's sake, immediately they stumble."

"Now these are the ones sown among thorns; they are the ones who hear the word, and the cares of this world, the deceitfulness of riches, and desires for other things entering in choke the word, and it becomes unfruitful."
"But these are the ones sown on good ground, those who hear the word, accept it, and bear fruit: some thirty fold, some sixty, and some hundred."

Mark 4:3-20

As Christians we are called to be the farmers, sowing the seeds of God's Word into one anothers lives and the world.

My Personal Testimony

Back in November of 1997, my spiritual journey began when God got my attention...

Suddenly, I was awakened out of a deep sleep. The clock read 3:15 am. I had two small children at the time and didn't want to wake them so, I decided to silently walk downstairs.

As I went into the dining room, I turned on the television set to the Trinity Broadcast Network. Jesse Duplantis was speaking and he was just finishing up a sermon on his "divine appointment" with God. He told his listeners that we all have a divine assignment given to each of us *from the moment He formed us in our mother's womb.* I said to myself, "I would love to hear the entire message some day."

As I turned off the television, I slowly began to walk into the kitchen. Suddenly, I stopped, dropped to my knees and began to cry. My cries quickly turned into uncontrollable sobs. As I was on my knees crying, a quiet, audible voice spoke to me and said,

1

"You're trying to please everyone, the only person you need to please is Me, but before I can "fill your vessel," you need to "empty it of yourself."

I was confused and afraid. Who was speaking to me? Why was I crying? "Fill my vessel?" "Empty it of myself?" It didn't make sense. I quietly walked back upstairs to my room, shut the door and fell asleep.

The next morning when I awoke, I decided not to share the experience I had the night before. Fear had set in. Thoughts of not being believed and the criticism that would follow made me even more afraid. I needed to keep it between myself and God. But as the days went on, I had a strong passion to read the Bible. I never had a desire to read the Bible in the past, but now I couldn't put it down. As the days turned into weeks, my spiritually blind eyes began to slowly open. As I read I asked God for knowledge and wisdom which can be found in **Colossians 1:10 & James 1:5.** I wanted the knowledge to continue reading God's Word and have the understanding to know what I was reading. I also asked for wisdom to not only read and understand, but to listen and hear when the Holy Spirit was speaking to me. I needed to

2

know how God's Word pertained to my life. The Bible teaches that in Christ are "hidden all the treasures of wisdom and knowledge."

As the years went by, I learned that my life was full of unknown *pride*. I was sitting on the throne of my life but the Holy Spirit was at my feet. I still wanted to be in control. The Holy Spirit was trying to tell me that "my vessel" needed to be "emptied" of this pride, so He could begin to "fill it" with with His Spirit and the Truth of God's Word.

I also learned that God cannot fill a "dirty vessel" which is still full of "self". With this understanding, I began my journey, a quest, to learn more about the Holy Spirit and the promises God had for me. Now I rely on God's Holy Spirit living inside of me to give me the strength to accomplish God's purposes in my life. I've chosen to surrender my life to the Holy Spirit and now He is on the throne of my life and I am kneeling at His feet. I now know that He, the Holy Spirit, was speaking to me on that early November morning back in 1997. In those early years, starting out as a "Baby Christian," the Holy Spirit began to speak to my heart through the Words of the Bible. God began to renew my mind and heart once I learned who I was in Christ.

While walking on my spiritual journey, the Holy Spirit began to fill my now emptied "vessel" to the brim and years later, it is overflowing with the Truth of God's Word. I am no longer a "people pleaser" but live each day to please Him. I've learned that without faith it is impossible to please God. My divine assignment, given to me from the moment I was conceived, is to be a witness for Him by sharing:

The Truth of God's Word,
The Good News of the Gospel
and to build the Kingdom one soul at a time.
All wisdom is found in the Holy Scriptures, yet
few seek the Truth.

I started walking on my spiritual journey when I
began reading the Word, starting in
The Gospel of John.

The Gospel of John

In the beginning was
The Word...

Verse 1 *In the beginning was **the Word**, and **the Word** was with God, and **the Word** was God.*

Verse 2 ***He** was in the beginning with God.*

Verse 3 *All things were made through **Him**, and without **Him** nothing was made that was made.*

Verse 4 *In **Him** was life, and the life was the **Light** of men.*

Verse 5 *And the **Light** shines in the darkness, and the darkness did not comprehend it.*

Verse 6 *There was a man sent from God, whose name was John.*

Verse 7 *This man came for a witness, to bear witness of the **Light**, that all through **Him** might believe.*

Verse 8 He was not that **Light**, but was sent to bear witness of the **Light**,

Verse 9 that was the true **Light** which gives **Light** to every man coming into the world.

Verse 10 **He** was in the world, and the world was made through **Him**, and the world did not know **Him**.

Verse 11 **He** came to his own, and **His** own did not receive **Him**.

Verse 12 But as many as received **Him**, to them **He** gave the right to become children of God, to those who believe in **His** name,

Verse 13 Who were born, not of blood, nor of the will of the flesh, nor of the will of man, but of God.

Verse 14 And **the Word** became flesh and dwelt among us, and we beheld **His** glory, the glory as of the only begotten of the Father, full of grace and truth.

Let us stop and pause here for a moment, and examine the Old Testament. The entire Old Testament points to Jesus' coming. Listed below are eight scriptures taken from the Old Testament predicting the coming of Christ, the long awaited Messiah.

Psalms 22:16-18   Micah 5:2
Isaiah 7:14   Zachariah 9:9
Zachariah 12:10   Isaiah 9:6
Isaiah 50:6

"But He was wounded for our transgressions, He was bruised for our iniquities; the chastisement for our peace was upon Him, and by His stripes we are healed."
Isaiah 53:5

Here Isaiah is clearly referring to Jesus and the severe beatings he endured before his crucifixion. How was he able to predict the crucifixion and death of Jesus hundreds of years before these events took place? The book of Isaiah was written around 700 B.C. When I went back and read those scriptures my eyes began to open and realize how Jesus was spoken about many years before he was born.

There are many Old Testament prophecies about the coming of Jesus Christ.

Let's go back to the beginning of John's gospel by inserting the word *"Jesus"* in place of the phrases, *The Word", "He", and "Him"*

Verse 1 "In the beginning was *Jesus*, and *Jesus* was with God, and *Jesus* was God.

Verse 2 *Jesus* was in the beginning with God.

Verse 3 and all things were made through *Jesus*, and without *Jesus* nothing was made that was made.

Verse 4 In *Jesus* was life, and the life was the life of men.

Verse 10 *Jesus* was in the world, and the world was made through *Jesus,* and the world did not know *Jesus.*

Verse 11 *Jesus* came to His own, and His own did not receive *Jesus.*

Verse 12 But as many as received *Jesus*, to them *Jesus* gave the right to become children of God, to those who believe in *Jesus'* name,

Verse 14 And *Jesus* became flesh and dwelt among us, and we beheld *Jesus'* glory, the glory of the only begotten of the Father, full of truth and grace."

Reading this I realized Jesus Christ is the Word and the creator of life. His light brings life to mankind. Although Christ created the world, the people he created didn't recognize him. Even the Jewish people, chosen by God to prepare the rest of the world for the Messiah, rejected him.

"He was in the world, and the world was made through Him, and the world did not know Him."
John 1:10

"If you had known Me, you would have known My Father also; and from now on you know Him because you have seen Him."
John 14:7

In verses 5,7,8, and 9 Jesus is referred to as being the Light.

> *"I have come as a light into the world, that whoever believes in Me should not abide in darkness."*
> **John 12:48**

Even though we live in a dark and evil world Jesus tells us that He is the Light who has come into the World and we who abide in Him will not live in darkness. Let Jesus, who is the light, direct your path.

Let us go back to the beginning and look at the life of Jesus in **Matthew 1:18.** Jesus was born in Bethlehem and grew in wisdom, stature, and favor with God and man. Even though Jesus was born of the virgin Mary, through the Holy Spirit, which we read in **Matthew 1:23,** he was also God in the flesh. God became a man and dwelt among men. He was not part man and part God; he was completely human and completely divine. Christ is the perfect example of God in human form.

> *"I and My Father are One."*
> **John 10:30**

10

Spiritual Renewal and The New Birth

God became a man in Jesus so that Jesus could die for our sins. Jesus rose from the dead to offer salvation so all people, through spiritual renewal and rebirth, could be re-united with God in Heaven. In **John 3:5** Jesus told Nicodemus, a Pharisee, and a member of the ruling council called the Sanhedrin,

> *Jesus answered, "Most assuredly, I say to you, unless one is born of water and the Spirit, he cannot enter the kingdom of God."*
> ***John 3:5***

"Born of water and spirit could refer to the contrast between physical birth (water) and spiritual birth (spirit) or baptism (water) and spiritual birth (spirit). When one is baptized in water it is an outward act that represents an inward decision. I chose to bury my old lifestyle and begin a new life which pleases Jesus! It was a faith decision that shouted to the world "I'm a Christian now living for Christ!" Being born makes you physically alive, but being born of God makes you spiritually alive and puts you in God's family, a decision I knew I could only make for myself. Jesus was explaining the importance of spiritual birth, saying that people do not enter the Kingdom by living a good and holy life, but by being *spiritually reborn.*

> *"Most assuredly, I say to you, unless one is born again, he*
> ***cannot see the kingdom of God."***
> ***John 3:3***

When I read that scripture I said to myself, "What does it mean to be born-again?" I learned the reason I needed to be born-again is because I had never been spiritually born to begin with. When the Bible speaks of being "born again", it actually means "born a second time." I came to realize that I was born physically into this world, but I was born without the spirit of God in my soul. I was spiritually dead. Yes, God created me, but He gave me a free will to decide for myself where I wanted to spend eternity.

We have all fallen short of God's glory and everyone is equal in God's eyes. I was a sinner in need of a Savior and understood that God looks at the condition of my heart which is my spirit.

12

There is only one way to enter into God's Kingdom, and that is you must be born again and renew your "dead" spirit by receiving the Holy Spirit in your heart. By re-reading John 3:3 I now realized that being born again is a requirement for salvation, but you must also repent. Repentance is not just asking for forgiveness but a true repentant heart includes having a genuine hatred of sin. You will know when you have truly repented once you have not only chosen to turn away from your sinful lifestyle but also turn away from *practicing* sin. You will not want to go back to it because you love God and don't want to hurt Him. I could not say, "Yes, I believe" and still continued choosing to sin. This would have been a false repentance.

> *"That's why those who are still under the control of their sinful nature can never please God."*
> ***Romans 8:8***

Repentance was the first step to my spiritual growth and pleasing God. It opened the door of my heart for the Holy Spirit to move in and bring the right relationships into my life. When I repented, Jesus forgave me and enable me to enter into His Kingdom. By coming to this understanding that this can only be done through receiving God's Spirit, the Holy Spirit which allowed a change to take place within me. By surrendering to the Holy Spirit, He helped me to see my need to receive Jesus Christ as my Savior. By His shed blood He took away my sins and threw them as far as the east is from the west and never to be remembered again. He helps me to live a life that is right and pleasing to God.

> *"As far as the east is from the west, so far has he removed our transgressions from us."*
> **Psalms 103:12**
> *"And I will remember your sins no more."*
> **Hebrews 8:12**

God says we all have sinned and all are in need of a Savior. To be "saved" means that a **conversion** or a **God-produced change** takes place in a person due to Jesus being received into their heart. You can be a church member who believes they are truly saved yet lack a **true** conversion. By making a true conversion one looks back on his or her old lifestyle never to return to it. Many have not confessed Jesus as their personal Savior. He is the one true awaited Messiah. He came in the flesh, died on the cross, and God raised Him from the dead; and is alive today!

Guidance of the Holy Spirit

God is three persons in one, the Father, the Son, and the Holy Spirit. Using the example of an apple, you have the outer skin, the flesh of the apple, and the seeds. Together they are one apple. The Father is like the outer skin, the Son is like the flesh, and the seeds are the Holy Spirit. Together they are One, just like the example of the apple. In the beginning when Adam and Eve were created and walked with God, they were placed in the Garden of Eden. In this garden were many trees, but in the center of the garden was the tree of knowledge, the tree of good and evil. God strictly prohibited Adam and Eve to eat the fruit of that particular tree. But if they chose to eat the fruit they would die. Not die a physical death but a spiritual death. The serpent, the Devil, came to tempt Eve. Satan, at one time, was a chief angel named Lucifer, who not only rebelled against God but wanted to be God because of this he was thrown out of heaven. The serpent, Satan, tempted Eve by telling her to doubt God's goodness. He told her that God did not want her to be knowledgeable like He was and made her focus on the things she couldn't have.

> *"You shall not surely die. For God knows that in the day you eat of it your eyes will be opened, and you will be like God, knowing good and evil."*
> ***Genesis 3:4,5***

Eve had a choice to make. She chose to disobey God and listen to Satan's lies and ate the fruit which she then gave to her husband, Adam, which he also chose to eat. Adam and Eve were soon thrown out of the garden because they chose to disobey God. In doing so, they lost the guidance of the Holy Spirit who was guiding and living within them and they "died" spiritually. As descendants of Adam, we also have lost the guidance of the Holy Spirit. As I continued to read scripture I came to the understanding that if I was not filled with the Holy Spirit I was being controlled by my sinful nature or flesh.

> *"But you are not in the flesh but in the Spirit, if indeed the Spirit of God dwells in you. Now if anyone does not have the Spirit of Christ, he is not His."*
> ***Romans 8:9***

16

For The Wages of Sin Is Death

"For the wages of sin is death, but the free gift of
God is eternal life through
Christ Jesus our Lord."
Romans 6:23

As I continued to read I learned that through Adam and Eve's disobedience, sin entered the world. Sin is a sickness to the soul. Sin is a choice of our own will opposed to God's will. It is the use of our own knowledge to make decisions to go our own way instead of God's way. The foundation to all sin is **selfishness and pride** as opposed to godliness. Through pride one becomes blinded. We set in our minds and hearts to go another way with a bad attitude and a rebellious spirit. Pat Robertson mentions in his book, *"Steps to Revival",* that there are several types of pride: Pride of family, pride of finance and accomplishment, pride of material possessions, pride of nationality, pride of employment and position, pride of religious affiliation, and pride of knowledge and education.

17

I've listed a few scripture verses that refer to pride:

Psalm 119:21   *Proverbs 21:45*
Proverbs 8:13   *Proverbs 26:12*
Proverb 13:10   *Proverbs 27:2*
Proverbs 16:18   *1 Corinthians 10:12*

Sin is loving ourselves and preferring our own way. Pride is rebelling against God instead of loving Him; seeking to please ourselves and justifying our actions. God calls sin the "works of the flesh."

"Now the works of the flesh are evident, which are:
*adultery, fornication, uncleanness, lewdness, idolatry, sorcery, hatred, contentions, jealousies, outbursts of wrath, selfish ambitions, dissensions, heresies, envy, murders, drunkenness, revelries, and the like; of which I tell you beforehand, just as I also told you in the time past, that those who **practice** such things will not inherit the Kingdom of God."*

Galatians 5:19-21

You can not continue practicing sin. God hates sin. Using the name of God in vain when you are angry is as serious a sin as murder in God's eyes. Just as lusting is the same as adultery.

"But I say to you that whoever looks at a woman to lust after her has already committed adultery with her in his heart."
Matthew 5:28
"For whoever shall keep the whole law, and yet stumbles in one point, he is guilty of all."
James 2:10

I realized that all sin is equal in God's eyes, there is no sin greater than another. Sin is sin and has to be paid for. Because you nor I could ever begin to pay for sin, Jesus Christ, in our place, paid the price for our sin with His precious blood. Jesus was our Passover Lamb that was slain and sacrificed Himself for all of our sins.

"For the life of the flesh is in the blood, and I have given it to you upon the alter to make an atonement for your soul; for it is the blood that makes atonement for the soul."
Leviticus 17:11

19

To "atone for" means to make amends or wash away. The precious blood flowing through Jesus' veins was that of His heavenly Father. It cleansed me and provided forgivness for all of my past, present and future sins.

> *"And according to the law almost all things are purified with blood, and without the shedding of blood there is no forgiveness of sin."*
> ***Hebrews 9:22***

By the shedding of His blood on the cross, He accomplished salvation for everyone who believes in Him and who He truly is. For me, it became a choice, a personal decision. If this is also your choice your sins will be washed away, never to be remembered by God again. God's Word also says that I have been justified. Here are a few verses from scripture that refer to justification:

Isaiah 64:6   *Romans 6:23*
Romans 3:20,24,28   *Ephesians 2:1-10*
Romans 4:5   *Titus 3:7*
Romans 5:1,9

Justified means "just as if I had never sinned." Jesus paid the price for all sin with His life.

Asking Jesus Into Your Heart

As I continued walking on my journey through the Word, I came upon this verse,

> *"For by grace you have been saved through faith, and that not of yourselves, it is the gift of God, not of works, lest anyone should boast."*
> ***Ephesians 2:8-9***

I came to the realization that I have been saved by grace through faith alone in Jesus Christ. I understood that I could not merit or do any good works to earn my salvation since it was a free gift . When a person is given a Christmas gift that person did nothing to earn that gift. If you are trying to *earn* your salvation by doing good works you are trying to achieve righteousness by your own merit. However, it is only through the blood sacrifice that Jesus made for us on the cross that we become righteous. To be righteous means you are now in *right-standing* before God but by trying to earn your *"right standing before God"* you becomes self-righteous. The Bible says in Isaiah 64:6 that in the eyes of God *"all our righteous acts are like filthy rags"* but *after* you are saved, by the gift of grace coupled together with faith, your good works will soon follow in every thought, word and deed. This will show your new love for Christ and that you are now living to please Him *by* your works. Scripture tells us these two truths, *"Faith without works is dead"* and *"works without faith is dead"* **James 2:14-26**. When you have real faith it will lead to real works. We will all spend eternity somewhere. I chose heaven to be my Eternal home. I knew the decision was mine to make and needed to work out my own salvaltion since I now had come to the understanding of what was required of me.

Have you chosen where you would like to spend eternity? If your answer is Heaven, God wants to prepare you now to receive His Holy Spirit, the guiding Spirit, that lived inside of Adam and Eve when they walked with God in the beginning of time. On the next page is a simple prayer. If you choose to say this prayer you're making the decision to repent, bury your old lifestyle and surrender your life and receive Jesus as your Lord and Savior. You may ask yourself, "Will He hear me?" Absolutely! He loves you and He's been waiting for you to come to Him. I encourage you to recite the following prayer and say it with meaning in your heart.

Pray this simple prayer out loud:

Heavenly Father, I may not understand all of this, but I know I need You to come into my heart and show me the Truth. I acknowledge that I am a sinner in need of a Savior. My sins have not only hurt you but others; I've also hurt myself. I truly repent and turn away from my old lifestyle of sin.
I believe that your Son Jesus died on the cross, shed His Blood for the forgiveness of my sins and rose again on the third day and is
alive today!

I want you to send your Holy Spirit to come live inside of me, helping me to change my life. I choose to surrender and receive your free gift of salvation through Your saving grace. I want to follow, obey, and put my trust in you, starting today, as my Lord and Savior.

In Jesus Name, Amen.

> *"This means that anyone who belongs to Christ has become a new person. The old life is gone; a new life has begun!"*
>
> **2 Corinthians 5:17**

If you have believed in Jesus for the first time or rededicated your life back to Christ, write your name and today's date on the blank lines as a record of the time of your salvation.

Name:_____

Date:_____

Time:_____

By praying this prayer and asking Jesus into your heart as your Lord and Savior not only have you become a child of God but you have also chosen to invite Jesus' precious Spirit, the Holy Spirit, to come live inside of you, giving you the strength and guidance you'll need to change your lifestyle and start a whole new life! By receiving the Holy Spirit He will produce in you the fruits of the Spirit.

> *"He will produce in you love, joy, peace, patience, kindness, faithfulness, goodness, gentleness and self-control, which are the fruits of the Spirit."*
> **Galatians 5:22**

> *"Abide in me, and I will abide in you. As a branch cannot produce fruit of itself, unless it abides in the vine, neither can you, unless you abide in me. I am the vine, you are the branches. He who abides in Me, and I in Him, bears much fruit; for without Me you can do nothing,"*
> **John 15:4-5**

To abide means to "live in". My "empty vessel" has been filled with His spirit, the Holy Spirit who now lives in me!

> *"Now He who has prepared us for this very thing is God, who also has given us His Spirit as a guarantee."*
> **2 Corinthians 5:5**

A guarantee of what?

A guarantee that you are saved and now can be sure that you will enter into the Kingdom of Heaven! In his book, **Laying the Foundation,** a bible study written by James Lee Beals, on page 323 tells us,

> *"Those who die in sin and without God will continue forever in this state. Whatever we have become at the time of judgment, we will be for eternity."*

We will not be given a second chance to receive salvation after we pass from this life to the next. God wants to do great things in us and He will if we'll let Him, but because we've been given free will He will not force any of this upon us. We are free to choose. Now I know that my complete salvation is by grace through faith in Jesus Christ, not by any good works, it is a gift from God. I believe that by the shedding of His blood for the forgiveness of sins, dying on the cross and being raised from the dead by the power of the Holy Spirit on the third day is not only the Good News but the simple foundation of the Christian faith.

In the beginning of my book I told you I found a treasure, that treasure was receiving the Holy Spirit through the truth of God's Word. I now know that I truly belonged to God, who I am in Christ, and given His Holy Spirit, who not only lives in me but produces the fruit of Jesus' spirit through me. He continues to help me with understanding of the Bible which continues to guide me and keep me on the right path. Now is the time to make sure you are on the narrow path that leads to Heaven and not on the broad path that leads to destruction.

Begin a new relationship with Jesus and start walking on your Spiritual Journey today!

Many Blessings,

Helen

"*Trust in the Lord with all your heart, and lean not on your own understanding;*
In all your ways acknowledge Him,
And He shall direct your path."
Proverbs 3:5-6

Have you ever wanted to share your faith and belief with others but didn't know what to say or where to start? I encourage you to "plant your seed" and support my ministry, The Holy Spirit Ministry, by purchasing a copy of my book and giving it to a friend or family member who is searching for the Truth in God's Word.

My ministry is to "plant the seed" into peoples lives through the Truth found in Scripture; to build The Kingdom of God one soul at a time.

Mark 4:3-20

Purchase your copy today!
Visit: **www.lulu.com/buy**
Enter: Helen V. Dugan

My Personal Testimony
By: Jorge Rudes

This is my story that God put in my life to touch people's hearts.
By Jorge Rudes

Here's my story involving the New Jesus Fish and Cross ® Art design. Let me share with you and to the world how God has changed my life and is continuing to use me for His glory. The two gifts given to me by God are of the arts and dreams. Four years ago, through many tears, I asked God to not only use me but show me how I could be used for His glory and His Love. I had no idea that He would hear and answer my prayers, but He sure did! I soon cried myself to sleep and He showed me in a dream (a vision) of my past and present both at the same time.

I saw myself walking on the sand back in Brazil were I was born and grew up. I noticed a boy drawing something in the sand. I looked over and it was an image of a fish, but not just any fish so I walked closer to take a better look. Wow! I thought. Just then the boy turned around, as if he was expecting me to be there, he said, **"the message is within the fish"** which is a reflection of Christ's Love. Just then I looked at the boy's face and realized it was me at the age of 7!   Just then I woke up and immediately I started drawing this fish. But this fish was not just any fish, it was **"the message within the fish"** that made it so special.

The fish was composed of a heart which forms the head, the number 7 drawn in the center of the fish, and completing the picture a Cross, which makes the tail.

I was so awestruck by the picture I saw drawn by the little boy (me) in my dream that it is now forever in my memory and has become my passion, my mission to this world.
Another message of the fish is:

"God's Perfect Gift"

My life's journey is one of adversity, courage, determination and faith.

30

My life wasn't easy growing up in an orphanage. The conditions of the orphanage was at times cruel and harsh. Even those who at the young age of three had to "work" to keep their stay until they were adopted. The lack of proper clothing, shoes and loving care has always stuck with me. Some of them were never adopted and were forced out of the orphanage on the day we turned 18 years of age to fend for themselves. Many didn't make it. They ended up dead or committing suicide. Some turned to drugs or gangs to ease their pain or to just simply fit in and feel loved. I'm sadden when I look back at that time in my life when I wished I had this fish to show and share God's true Love on the Cross But God had bigger and better plans for me, it just wasn't the right time.

My past is a memory of hardships and pain but not a memory that leads to bitterness. It is my catalyst to give back!I'm not sure where this symbol and its message will lead me, but I do know that we are in the last days and now more than ever we are to stand up for what we believe in and go into the world to show God's Love !! Whether it is by a symbol, art work, singing, missions, or even being a pastor, we need to make a stand for Our Lord Jesus Christ who gave Himself as the Perfect Gift on the Cross so we could obtain salvation and live with Him FOREVER !! God has given me this mission and it has become my soul purpose in life. I want to make sure that I am doing God's will by showing the world The New Jesus Fish and sharing my stories in hope they too may have eternal life with Him and also have the opportunity to spread God's Love through The New Jesus Fish with whom ever they meet in their life's journeys.

My hope is to one day help children and orphans in Brazil. My passion is to help change the life's of people and their families with water, food, clothes, and shelter. these are needed just to survive. If it takes all I have to make this happen I'll live to my death to do so!! I want to give others hope by showing God's Love. This is what we were BORN TO DO which will enable us all to have a better future. I would also like to give 7% of every dollar back to the orphans in Brazil and the balance of the money I will share with all those who need it and not just those who want it. This is my destiny and my life !!!

Thank you for letting me share my testimony with you. Please help me by spreading my story and sharing this symbol of Love.

The New Jesus Fish is a Reflection
of God's Greatest Gift,
His Son Jesus Christ.

Out of God's Love, unto us His Son was Born as a
Man who is our
Savior Jesus Christ.
Jesus said,

**"Follow Me And I will Make You
Fishers of men."**

God's Love is so Perfect! He's the giver of Life.
God's-Perfect-Gift is a Symbol of LOVE, and
through my dream the
New Jesus Fish was Born.

www.thenewJesusfish.com

http://www.youtube.com/watch?
v=3UuN53No4BA
http://www.youtube.com/watch?
v=0NyNxOFgAf0&feature=mfu_in_order&list=U
L
May God richly bless you,
Jorge

"All Scripture is inspired by God and is useful to teach us what is true and to make us realize what is wrong in our lives. It corrects us when we are wrong and teaches us to do what is right. God uses it to prepare and equip His people to do every good work."
2 Timothy 3:16-17

If your body does not receive daily food and drink it will eventually die, the same is true with your new spiritual body. Your new spiritual life, as well as your physical life needs nourishment. In John 6:35, it tells us Jesus is the Bread of Life and this nourishment is God's Word, which will help you grow spiritually. The last chapter of my book will encourage you to begin your journey through the Word by reading your Bible and highlighting other verses from the Gospel of John. Begin to renew your heart but first you must renew your mind by learning who you are in Christ!

Verses from the Gospel of John

Eternal Life Through Jesus

John 3:15-16
John 3:36
John 4:14
John 5:24
John 6:35
John 6:51

John 8:12
John 8:24
John 10:9
John 11:25
John 14:6

Do You Know Who You Are In Christ?

I AM ACCEPTED

John 1:12
I am God's child.

John 15:15
I am Christ's friend.

Romans 5:1
I have been justified.

1 Corinthians 6:17
I am united with the Lord, and I am one spirit with Him.

1 Corinthians 6:19,20
I have been bought with a price. I belong to God.

1 Corinthians 12:27
I am a member of Christ's body.

Ephesians 1:1
I am a saint.

Ephesians 1:5
I have been adopted as God's child.

Ephesians 2:18
I have direct access to God through the Holy Spirit.

Colossians 1:14
I have been redeemed and forgiven of all my sins.

Colossians 2:10
I am complete in Christ.

I AM SECURE

Romans 8:1-2
I am free forever from condemnation.

Romans 8:28
I am assured that all things work together for good.

Romans 8:31-34
I am free from condemning charges against me.

Romans 8:35-39
I cannot be separated from the love of God.

2 Corinthians 1:21,22
I have been established, anointed and sealed by God.

Philippians 1:6
I am confident that the good work that God has begun in me will be perfected.

Philippians 3:20
I am a citizen of heaven.

Colossians 3:3
I am hidden with Christ in God.

2 Timothy 1:7
I have not been given a spirit of fear but of power, love and a sound mind.

Hebrews 4:16
I can find grace and mercy to help in time of need.

1 John 5:18
I am born of God; the evil one cannot touch me.

I AM SIGNIFICANT

Matthew 5:13-14
I am the salt and the light of the earth.

John 15:1-8
I am a branch of the true vine, a channel of His life.

John 15:16
I have been chosen and appointed to bear fruit.

Acts 1:8
I am a personal witness of Christ.

1 Corinthians 3:16
I am God's temple.

2 Corinthians 5:17-21
I am a minister of reconciliation for God.

Ephesians 2:6
I am seated with Christ in the heavenly realm.

Ephesians 3:12
I may approach God with freedom and confidence.

Recommended Books to Read

Devotional
Smith Wigglesworth
Amazon.com

The Purpose Driven Life
Rick Warren
saddlebackresources.com

True and False Conversion
Ray Comfort
livingwaters.com

Battlefield of the Mind
Joyce Meyer
joycemeyer.org

Laying the Foundation
James Lee Beall
A Full Bible Study
alibris.com

The Spirit-Filled Life
Charles Stanley
Intouch.org

Notes

*In **Psalms 139:13-16** David reminds us,*

*"For You created my inter most being; You knit me together in my mother's womb. I praise You because I am fearfully and wonderfully made; Your works are wonderful.
I know that full well.*

My frame was not hidden from You when I was made in the secret place. When I was woven together in the depths of the earth, your eyes saw my unformed body.

All the days ordained for me were Written in your Book before one of them came to be."

*"My precious child, I love you
very much."*

Jesus

41